# Teddy Bear

## IN THE WONDER LAND

COLORING BOOK

*ART DESIGN AND STRESS RELIEVING PATTERNS*

# LOVE PANDA



Printed in The U.S.A.

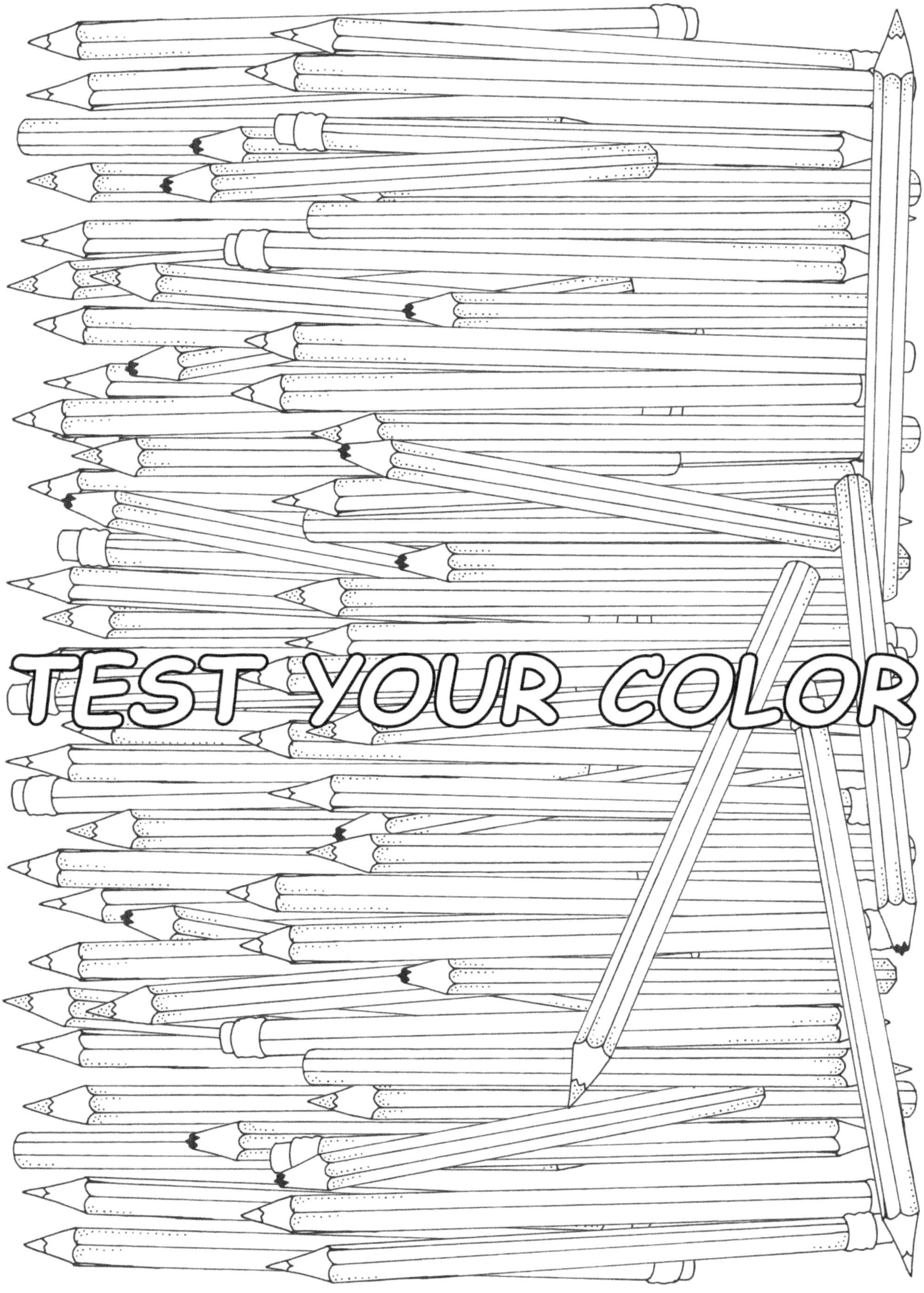
TEST YOUR COLOR

1.

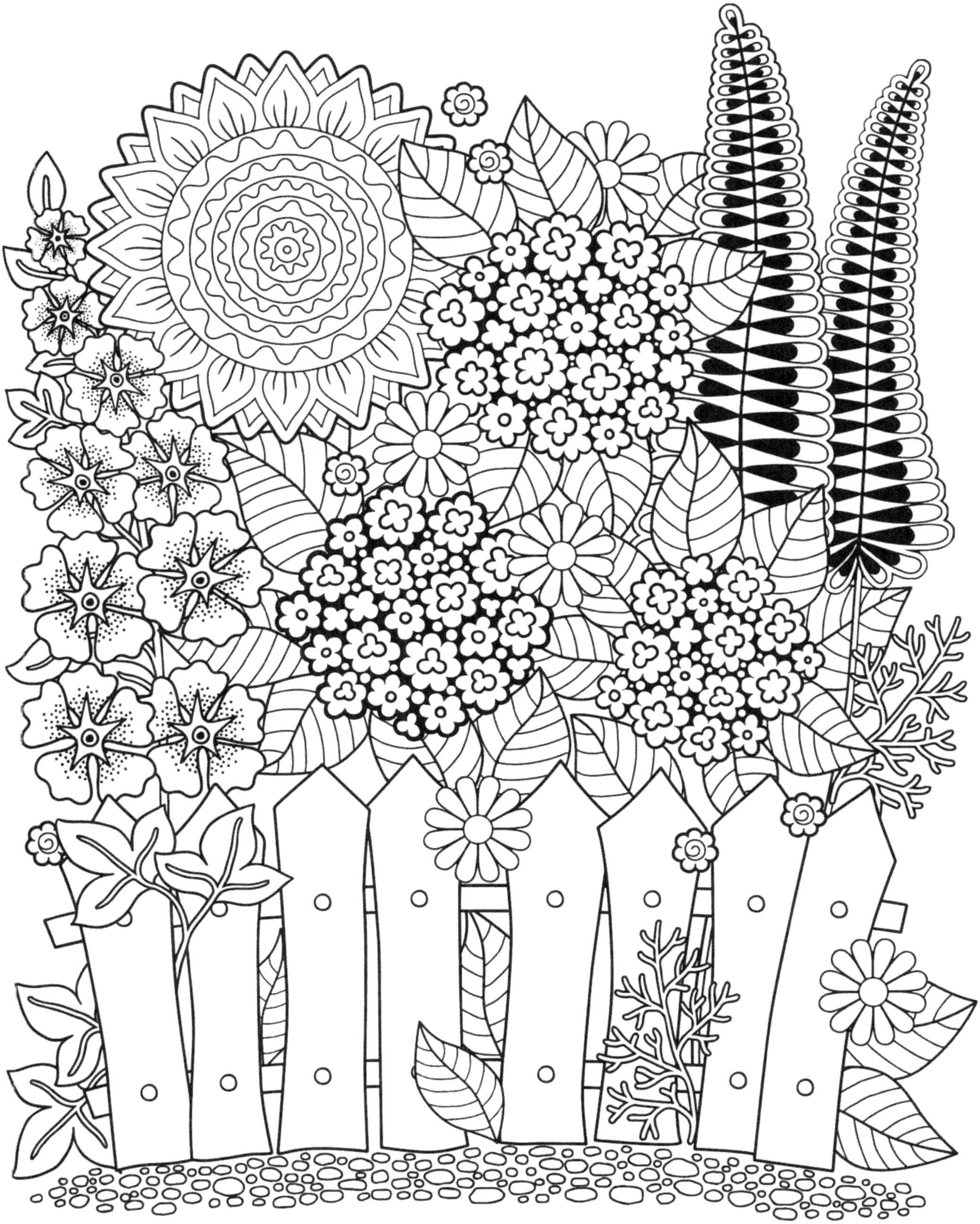

www.ingramcontent.com/pod-product-compliance
Lightning Source LLC
Chambersburg PA
CBHW081420280526
45788CB00009B/3176
*9781545232088*